Nourish your Soul

Dorothy K. Ederer O.P.

NEW PRIORY PRESS

EXPLORING THE DOMINICAN VISION

Mary!
You're a beautiful
woman of God!
Love
Sr. Dorothy
Ederer

Dedication

I dedicate this book to my parents:
Ann and Bernard Ederer,
who always nourished my soul
and also to my siblings and their spouses, Carol and Bob,
Bernard and Judy, Gerrie and Joe,
Fr. John, Jeanne and Julie.
In addition, I want to dedicate this book to
my nieces and nephews and their spouses:
Colleen and Rob, Jenny and Martin,
John Patrick and Shannon, Cheri and Larry, David and Jenny,
Eugene and Nikki, and Eddie and Judi;
and to my grandnieces and grandnephews Mallory, Bryce,
Helena, Katlyn, Kayleigh, Hannah, Bradney, RJ, and Jacob.

Acknowledgement

I could not have had this book published without the help of my Dominican brothers: Fr. Andy McAlpin, whose encouragement and support is always well timed, and Fr. Albert Judy and Terry Jarbe who worked diligently to prepare the manuscript for print.

A special thanks to Gary Pearce who took the photo and for Kelly Sandula-Gruner who transformed it into an exquisite cover. Madeline Carino added her special touch by contributing the graphic designs in the book.

Words cannot express my gratitude to Jan Grabinski and Jean Shane, whose expertise in proofreading this manuscript was invaluable.

I also want to thank Fr. Joseph F. Girzone for his continual support and encouragement.

vi

Foreword

In these busy days with life's pressures squeezing every minute of our precious time, it is hard to steal even a few minutes to pray, to say nothing of doing a whole meditation. The most we can do every so often during the day is just close our eyes, place ourselves in God's presence and enjoy the moment knowing we are both there for each other.

Even though it is not easy to meditate, or even come up with a thought that may cheer us up in a stressful predicament, or a brilliant idea to help solve a pressing problem, the Minute Meditations in this charming **Nourish Your Soul** treasure will calm our high speed minds, and put life's disjointed events into clear and healthy perspective.

Fr. Joseph F. Girzone
Author of the "Joshua" books

"Be consistent in your dedication
to showing your
gratitude to others.
Gratitude is a fuel, a medicine,
and spiritual and emotional
nourishment."
Steve Maraboli

Contents

"When you recover or discover
something that nourishes your
soul and brings joy,
care enough about yourself to
make room for it in your life."

Jean Shinoda Bolen

"No one has ever become poor by giving."

Anne Frank

Words to Ponder: You cannot outdo God in generosity. I remember, while working in New York, we wrote a check for a young man who needed help to pay for his wife's tuition to go to college. The check was for $1,500. It was practically all we had left in our checking account, and we had bills to pay that week. I kept hearing, "Trust in God." The next morning when I opened the mail, there was an envelope from Doubleday, and inside was a check for $100,000. The money was for a three year contract for desk calendars with quotes from his Joshua books. I stopped dead in my tracks. I showed it to Fr. Joseph. He smiled and said, "I told you we can never outdo God in generosity." This poem expresses what it means to have a generous heart.

A Generous Heart

A sure way to be joyful is to be generous.
Instead of worrying about what you can get,
enjoy giving all you can give.
Living generously is living well and living richly.
It makes you an active participant not only in your own good fortune,
but also in the good fortune of others.

1

Life can be an incredibly beautiful and wonderful experience.
Your generosity magnifies that beauty and wonder many times over.

Generosity is not merely a matter of material offerings.
Real and meaningful generosity is giving of yourself.

Give your love, your attention, your compassion,
your interest, curiosity and genuine caring.
Give your time, your understanding, your peaceful,
positive presence and your commitment.

Live each day with a generous heart.
Make life's abundance even more abundant
by giving the best that you have.

Ralph Marston

God Whispered: Relax. I want you to continue being generous. You need to learn how to trust more in my love and concern for your well-being. I know precisely what your needs are and I will take care of them. You will experience my unwavering love for you. I always listen to your requests. Continue to give to others and don't worry. I will not let you down.

"A hero is somebody who is selfless, who is generous in spirit, who just tries to give back as much as possible and help people. A hero to me is someone who saves people and who really deeply cares."

Debi Mazar

Words to Ponder: Who is a hero in your life? We all have a hero; my dad was one of mine. I remember, when I was young, he walked with me to the grove of evergreen trees in our back yard. Putting his arm around me, he said, "Dort, see those evergreen trees? As the leaves on the other trees fall away and die, these trees stay alive and green all through the winter. It is like God's love. It never changes. It is unwavering and unconditional, and ever present." Looking at me he said, *"Dort, it is also like my love for you. Things around you may change, but my love for you will always be the same, ever unchanging. You may do things I do not like, but I will always love you."* Since then, I have never looked at an evergreen tree without thinking about my dad and God's unconditional love for me.

God Whispered: I want you to be a hero who will reflect my love and compassion. I want you to be there for others in need. Continue to serve with a generous and selfless heart. I will share your joy and multiply it.

"Sometimes I think I'm the luckiest person in the world. There's nothing better than having work you really care about. Sometimes I think my greatest problem is lack of confidence. I'm scared, and I think that's healthy."

Jane Fonda

Words to Ponder: This quote resonates with me. While a part of me knows that I am very blessed, I still vacillate sometimes as I lack the confidence I need to accomplish something. I may even think I'm not good enough or worry that I don't do things the correct way. The one thing for certain I do know is that I am loved by a God who understands me and encourages me not to give up. I know we all have insecurities but we also need the willingness to start over and keep trying. Insecurities can help us depend on God more and less on ourselves.

God Whispered: I am blessed to have someone who desires to give without counting the cost. I know you have insecurities. I want you to depend on me more and less on yourself. When you feel insecure, you turn to me. That makes me happy. You know that I am always there for you. Never doubt my love for you.

"One of the most calming and powerful actions you can do to intervene in a stormy world is to stand up and show your soul. Struggling souls catch light from other souls who are fully lit and willing to show it."

Clarissa Pinkola Estés

Words to Ponder: When I am struggling, I like to be around people who are happy and generous as I want to be more like them. David Haas wrote the song: "Come Live in the Light." It is about people who show mercy and let their light touch others. When we are walking with God and living in the light, we attract others like ourselves. We begin to realize that we can accomplish anything as long as we continue walking with God. When we ignore someone who is different, we cut ourselves off from a part of life. Instead we need to remain open and ready for anything or anyone that comes our way and respond with trust and hope.

God Whispered: I want you to absorb deeply the light that shines on you. I will fill your spirit with a love that will drive out any fear or anxiety that you have. When you are happy, I rejoice. I will always be faithful to my promises. My desire is for you to be a reflection of me by the way you treat and care for others.

"Never forget that you are one of a kind. Never forget that if there weren't any need for you in all your uniqueness to be on this earth, you wouldn't be here in the first place. And never forget, no matter how overwhelming life's challenges and problems seem to be, that one person can make a difference in the world. In fact, it is always because of one person that all the changes that matter in the world come about. So be that one person. "

R. Buckminster Fuller

Words to Ponder: Don't we all want to be a person who can make the world a better place? When we approach life with a giving heart, we usually experience a sense of fulfillment and we are rarely disappointed. In Matthew West's song "Do Something," he sings about all the problems in our world, and he asks God to do something about them. God's response was, "That's why I created you." We are responsible for each other. When we see all the needs, we realize that we have to take a stand, and do something that will make a difference.

God Whispered: It brings joy to my heart when you put your love into action. It is one thing to see the needs around you, but when you forget yourself and do something for another, it makes me happy.

"What we find in our soulmate is not something wild to tame, but something wild to run with."

Robert Brault

Words to Ponder: We all search for a soulmate, someone who shares the same morals, and values we do. We desire someone to love us, as we are, without expectations. A soulmate also relates to us on a spiritual level. This relationship becomes deeper than that of a good friend. Once we find a soulmate, we feel more complete. We keep searching until we find someone with these qualities. Far too often, we settle for someone because we are afraid that we can't do better. Be patient. God has someone special for you, someone who deserves you.

God Whispered: You love challenges and adventure. I know the desires of your heart; you can't hide anything from me. I know your thoughts before you speak them. I made you that way. I love you more than you can imagine. I will be with you in every challenge you take on and every adventure you decide to tackle. Invite me into your fun times. I will help you find your soulmate.

"Faith is the seamstress who mends our torn belief, who sews the hem of childhood trust and clips the threads of grief."

Joan Walsh Anglund

Words to Ponder: My mom taught me how to sew. As a seamstress, I enjoyed making something beautiful out of remnants. I would gather all the pieces of fabric and try to create something unique and lovely. I have made quilts, suits, dresses, and skirts. After a project was finished, I looked at it and rejoiced in what I had created. My mom also taught me how to pray. She had a holy hour every morning. "I give my first hour to God, then my family and friends." Looking back, I realize that sewing is a lot like our faith. We gather all the things we have been taught by our parents and our church, and then we try to put it all in proper perspective. At times, even though it may not totally make sense, we still know that it is good. We continue to believe and trust that God can take anything and make it into something beautiful. We just need to be open and allow it to happen.

God Whispered: Your faith may falter at times but know that I am here always to guide you and help you put all those torn or broken pieces together into something beautiful. You live your faith by caring for others and helping those who are broken to be whole again.

"Show me someone who has done something worthwhile, and I'll show you someone who has overcome adversity."

Lou Holtz

Words to Ponder: When Fr. Joseph F. Girzone wanted to get his first book **Joshua** published, the publisher told him, "Books like that don't sell." He was so determined to have it published, that he started his own publishing company and sent out his book to all his friends. His friends loved the book and spread the word to everyone they knew. One day, the president of Curtis Brown Agency called him and said: *"I read your book and was deeply touched. I want to be a part of what that book does for people. If you need an agent, I would be more than happy to be yours!"*

His agent found a publisher for him and he is his agent to this day. Fr. Joe not only overcame adversity but went on to publish 27 books. A number of his books have been best sellers. His books have touched the hearts of millions of people.

God Whispered: I am proud that you never give up when faced with adversity. I didn't create you to give up on your dreams. I want you to make a difference in this world. I admire your dedication and determination. I will be with you all the way. You know you can always depend on me.

**"When I slow down long enough to smell the roses,
I usually see the beauty and all else that is ours to share."**

Morgan Jennings

Words to Ponder: I cannot begin to tell you how many times I have been told to slow down. The problem is that I don't want to, mainly because I don't want to miss anything. There are so many things to do and limited time to do them. I am sure you have heard that: "We only go around this way once, and we may never pass this way again." With that in mind: whatever we can experience, whatever we can accomplish, however we can help another, let's do it. Let's make each day a blessing.

God Whispered: Relax; I will give you the time that is needed to accomplish what I have planned for you. Trust in me and don't worry. I have plans for you that will not only give you hope, but also inspire you to give your time generously to others. Take some quiet time and listen to me. I will give you the desire of your heart.

"A complete reevaluation takes place in your physical and mental being when you've laughed and had some fun."

Catherine Ponder

Words to Ponder: We need to laugh at our mistakes. Laughter is contagious, it is the best medicine. It encourages wellness. When you can laugh with another, you help them heal. I spent a day with a friend of mine who has cancer and we laughed so hard. The next week the doctor said to her, "I don't know what you have done, but I see some changes." She was shocked. She told the doctor that a friend made her laugh most of the day. Laughter not only helps us mentally, but can also help us physically!

God Whispered: Remember that laughter recharges your body. It can activate every cell in your being. You come alive as I watch you laugh with your friends. You are energized, much happier, and more at peace. Emotionally you feel better about yourself. I want you to continue to find things to laugh about so that you are constantly being healed of anything that could cause your body harm.

**"I have learned that faith means trusting in advance
what will only make sense in reverse."**

Philip Yancey

Words to Ponder: As I ponder the things that have happened in my life, I realize that they only make sense to me after the fact. Every job I took, every person I met has affected my life - always for the better. The more I trust in God, the better my life runs. God is always faithful to God's promises.

God Whispered: I want you to have faith in my promises. I know the plans I have for you. They are plans for you to prosper, for you to do well and use the gifts and talents I have given you. When you put your trust in me, it always turns out better than when you try to do things on your own. I will lead you to places you have never dreamed of and to do things you never imagined you could do. Continue to have faith in my words and trust that I know the desire of your heart!

"Success is not the key to happiness. Happiness is not the key to success. If you love what you are doing, you will be successful."

Herman Cain

Words to Ponder: I have loved every job I have ever had because I was able to use the gifts and talents that God gave me. When you love what you do, you become more creative and eventually successful. Your enthusiasm can become contagious, giving life to those who work around you. Marshall Field had these **12 rules of Success**

Remember:

The value of time
The success of perseverance
The pleasure of working
The dignity of simplicity
The worth of character
The power of kindness
The influence of example
The obligation of duty
The wisdom of economy
The virtue of patience
The improvement of talent
The joy of originating

God Whispered: I want you to be happy at whatever you do. Life is to be lived and treasured. When I see you happy, I know you are using the gifts I gave you. You are successful when you allow me to be a part of what you do. Remember, I am your companion on any journey you take. Trust in me and turn to me. I am always there for you.

"Don't mix bad words with your bad mood. You'll have many opportunities to change a mood, but you'll never get the opportunity to replace the words you spoke."

Author Unknown

Words to Ponder: We need to think before we speak, to choose our words wisely, rather than react. Once we say something, we can't take it back, and if our words hurt someone, that's even worse. It is far better to walk away from a situation than to hurt someone by our words. If we know we are in a bad mood, we should at least warn those around us, so they won't take offense.

God Whispered: I know how you feel when you hurt someone. You beat yourself up for it. You are harder on yourself than I am. You keep going over and over the situation again and again in your mind. You try to correct or explain what you said that hurt the other person. While words can't be taken back, you can help heal the other by reaching out and asking for forgiveness. Everyone wants someone to care enough to ask for forgiveness. You will feel better if you at least try.

**"The kids who need the most love will ask for it
in the most unloving of ways."**

Author Unknown

Words to Ponder: Each child is unique and each has different gifts. Hopefully, as parents and teachers, we have learned that all children (and even siblings) are not alike and that we can't keep comparing our children (or students) to one another. In my family of seven children, we are all different. Some of us are more outgoing, while others are more reflective. Each child looks at life through their own lenses, often colored by their experiences. Some see things through rose-colored glasses and others see things through dark, fearful lenses. Most children crave attention. If we can give them positive attention, most of the time they will act in loving ways.

God Whispered: I created you all unique. Each one of you has special gifts that no one else has. I want you to use those gifts to reflect my presence to others. You are loved and cherished by me and I want you to know that. My love for you is endless. I will never give up on you. I may challenge you, but only with love! Speak kind and affirming words to children. They are innocent and crave to be loved by someone. Be that person.

**"Everything is so dangerous that nothing is
really very frightening."**

Gertrude Stein

Words to Ponder: Some people like to live dangerously, while others choose to live in fear. Fear can stop us from becoming the person God intended us to become. Every day we make choices to choose life or resist it. I prefer to be a risk taker. I choose life and all its challenges. I put my trust in a higher power and know I will learn something from every adventure.

God Whispered: I want you to trust in me. I will never lead you into a dangerous situation. Every situation will help you to grow if you remain open. I will continue to direct you as long as you put your trust in me. Ninety percent of the time, the things you imagine never happen. Keep trusting in me. Don't let fear control your life. Have faith.

"Toleration is the greatest gift of the mind."

Helen Keller

Words to Ponder: Learning to be tolerant isn't easy. We probably all have heard the expressions: "*We can't always change our situation, but we can always change our attitude,*" and, "*We can't change people, we can only love them.*" By accepting and loving people as they are, they often grow and change as a result of being loved. Loving others can help them become the best person they can be. Love can be healing. Knowing that, sometimes I still find it hard to tolerate the poor behavior of another. In situations like that, I try not to react, instead I choose to be kind. I also pray for them and remember what Jesus said about forgiveness. I want to live my life loving and caring for others.

God Whispered: I want you to continue to love others no matter how they treat you. When people are mean and disagreeable, it is because they are hurting, so don't take offense. Reach out and surprise them by doing something nice. Compliment them, affirm them, smile at them or pray for them. People can change when they feel loved and accepted. I want you all to be a reflection of me.

**"Feeling gratitude and not expressing it is like
wrapping a present and not giving it."**

Author Unknown

Words to Ponder: We were raised to thank people when they did something for us or gave us a gift. After constantly being reminded to thank others, it eventually became a habit. In our fast-paced world today, it seems most people are not even aware that they didn't say thank you. I want to take the time now to thank those who have supported me in my ministry. For the woman who helped me furnish all the rooms at St. John's Student center, for the women who bring cookies for our cookie jars and bags of candy for the students' lounges. It is only fitting that I share with you one of my favorite quotes, *"Let us be grateful to people who make us happy; they are the charming gardeners who make our souls blossom."* Marcel Proust

God Whispered: You will not always be thanked for what you do for others. Remember, not everyone feels the same way you do or was brought up the same way. Be true to yourself and do those things your parents taught you. I didn't create you to be like everyone else. You are unique and special. I want you to continue to be a faith-filled person. Do what you know is right. Always follow your heart and be honest with your thoughts.

"Too often we underestimate the power of a touch, a smile, a kind word, a listening ear, an honest compliment or the smallest act of caring, all of which have the potential to turn a life around."

Leo Buscaglia

Words to Ponder: So often we underestimate the power of our words or an honest compliment. We don't realize how much what we say or do affects another. A word of encouragement has inspired people to do great things. By hearing, "I believe in you, you can do it," inventions have been created and projects have been developed. Working with college students, affirmation went a long way. It gave confidence to believe in themselves. We all need someone to believe in us.

God Whispered: I know you better than you know yourself. I know you love to affirm others and make them happy. I gave you confidence to reach out to those who are in need of a kind word, a listening ear and an honest compliment. You have seen and experienced their reaction to acts of kindness. I love seeing my children supporting one another and helping them use their full potential.

"Let me remind you: Wherever your focus is directed, that is where your energy goes. Whatever you allow in your space, you eventually become."

Author Unknown

Words to Ponder: Are you using your energy to make this a better world? Perhaps you are questioning whether one person can really make a difference because our world needs so much. I believe each of us can make a difference especially when we put our gifts to work for the good of others. I enjoy using my energy to help others find, use and perfect their gifts and talents. Perhaps they are passionate about the homeless and use their organizational skills to plan a trip to Appalachia to repair homes or work with Habitat for Humanity. What are you passionate about? How can you use your energy and gifts to help others? What will your legacy be?

God Whispered: I want you to continue to find ways to use your time and energy to help others. Choose your friends wisely. Some may use you for their benefit, others may want you because of your personality or position. Always remain true to the person I created you to be. Continue to direct your energy by being kind to others.

"Be still and listen to the stillness within."

Darlene Larson Jenks

Words to Ponder: This quote reminds me of my favorite scripture passage, "Be still and know that I am God." It is only when I am still that I can hear what God is calling me to do. I pray, listen and wait. God has never failed to let me know where he wants me to go or what he wants me to do. When you are questioning what God is calling you to do, remember to take time to be still, pray, listen and wait.

God Whispered: I know you want to trust that I will lead you to a place where you will be free to use your gifts and talents. When you are free from outside noises and able to hear me whisper you will feel my presence in your life and be at peace. You will feel secure when you count on me to be your guide. While you desire to put your complete trust in me, at times you still waver and doubt. That is okay, because I know you will turn to me in confidence. Let go! I know your heart.

"She knew that she was formed by God's hands, dreamed up in his heart, and placed in this world for a purpose."

Author Unknown

Words to Ponder: What is your purpose in life? What do you think God has in mind for you? Do you believe you are living what you have been called to do? What is your dream? You have been called here for a particular purpose. While you may not know what your purpose is now, when you look back at your life, you will see the reason for your existence.

God Whispered: I knew before you were born what you would do with your life. I watched you as you listened to your inner voice. You never stopped listening and you continue to help others to listen to the voice within. All those whispers of love and affirmation were intentional. I will never leave you. I am here to help you in every circumstance. Just trust in me. I have not failed you.

**"Look closely at the present you are constructing.
It should look like the future you are dreaming."**

Alice Walker

Words to Ponder: The things you do with your life today will definitely affect your future. What are you creating for yourself? Are you using your gifts to their full potential? Do you help those in need? Are you respectful of those who are different? Do you give without expecting anything in return? Are you living your dream? Reflect on the words in this poem:

Dream

*You have everything you need to follow your **dream***
Just look in your heart and you'll find the confidence in yourself
that will make each challenge easier to face.
*You'll discover the **hope** that will keep you believing.*
*You'll find an inner **strength** that will help you past obstacles.*
*And you'll see the **happiness** that's waiting for you if you keep trying.*
*If you listen to your **heart** you'll reach your **dream.***

Terry Matz

God Whispered: The more you trust in me and let go, the more you will experience my love and guidance. Please let me be a part of your adventure. I see plans for you that will help you prosper. Trust that I will be with you every step of the way. I love it when I see you happy and successful. Never leave me out of your plans. I will be there to dream and create with you

"Two things to remember in life: Take care of your thoughts when you are alone, and take care of your words when you are with people."

Author Unknown

Words to Ponder: It is important to collect your thoughts and ponder what you may say to another. What we say reflects what is in our heart. Words can heal or hurt. When you are at peace with yourself, you can get along with just about anyone. However, if you are upset, angry, embarrassed, lonely, others will know it. Even though it is hard to cover up our feelings, we must keep control over the words we speak. We must always be considerate.

God Whispered: The more you call on me to help you, the more at peace you will become. You may be hurting and embarrassed but it is vital that you stay connected to me. I will give you good thoughts to think and the right words to speak. No matter what situation you are in I will always be there to guide you on the right path.

"Know your worth. Know when you have had enough and move on from the people who keep ruining your happiness."

Author Unknown

Words to Ponder: We have all been in situations where there are people who are difficult to work with or who are jealous of our accomplishments. We have to remember that it is their problem not ours. We are called to be thoughtful and kind. While we can't change people, if we can accept them as they are and treat them lovingly, they may change.

God Whispered: I know how difficult it can be to be around people who are jealous of the things you do. Look at my Son's life: he forgave people when they were weak, he healed people and made them whole, and people were still suspicious of his motives. It was jealously that made them kill him. Ignore pettiness. Move on and be the person I created you to be.

"No matter what happens, no matter how far you seem to be away from where you want to be, never stop believing that you will somehow make it. Have an unrelenting belief that things will work out, that the long road has a purpose, that the things that you desire may not happen today, but they will happen. Continue to persist and persevere."

Brad Gast

Words to Ponder: So often we try to do things on our own and only turn to God when things go wrong, or when things don't happen as we hoped or planned. At times we may want to give up, but we must be like the persistent widow in the bible [Luke 18:1-8], she never gave up on what she wanted. We must have that same determination, no matter how many distractions or setbacks happen. We have to stay focused on God and trust that he will never leave us.

God Whispered: I will continue to affirm you. I am always here for you no matter what may happen in your life. You have to stay focused on me. I have wonderful plans for you, but I will wait until you are ready to receive them. Even though you believe that some of your prayers have not been answered, you must learn to trust in me. You must learn patience. Go gently through your day trusting in me.

"Time is more valuable than money. You can get more money, but you cannot get more time."

Jim Rohn

Words to Ponder: A friend once told me, "Be picky with whom you invest your time, wasted time is worse than wasted money." Life is too short to spend time with people who have negative attitudes. Our tendency is to avoid people like this because they bring us down. While we are called to treat everyone we meet with kindness, choosing our friends wisely can help us have the type of life we want. We all want to be happy and live a full life. So choose those persons who lift your spirits and brighten your day.

God Whispered: I crafted you to be a "life giver" and to spend your time serving others. When you are around negative people, they bring you down and you have a tendency to limit your service. Turn to me when you feel down and I will lift you up. I am always here for you. Trust in me and continue to choose life!

"If you are always trying to be normal, you will never know how amazing you can be."

Maya Angelou

Words to Ponder: What does normal really mean? The free dictionary on line say normal means: *"Conforming to the standard or the ordinary type; usual; not abnormal; regular; natural."* It also means: *"Someone who is approximately average in any psychological trait, as in intelligence, personality, or emotional adjustment."* Don't you want to be a little abnormal, an individual, not like everyone else? Do you want to just blend in with the crowd? Or do you want to stand out as unique and special, the way God created you to be? Be true to the person God called you to be and you will do things you never dreamed were possible.

God Whispered: I created you all unique and special, but it seems that society puts pressure on you to be like everyone else. Please be true to the person I created you to be. Stand up for what you hold as pure, good, and honest. Make a difference. You will see how great life can be and how amazing you can be.

**"Fill your life with experiences, not things.
Have stories to tell, not stuff to show."**

Author Unknown

Words to Ponder: Coming from a family of nine, I don't remember us having much "stuff" as children. Our parents were all about creating memories instead! The events that I still remember are the vacations we had together as family. It seems whenever we get together, we talk about the wonderful vacations we had and the good times we had with each other. To this day, we can still reminisce and entertain each other with stories. I don't ever recall us talking about the "things" we got unless it was something out of the ordinary. The time we spent with family and friends is the most valuable treasure of all. For these experiences are what we remember.

God Whispered: I want you to bask in my love and remember all the wonderful events that have happened in your life. Remember the good times, the surprises, the events that drew you closer to me and the people you saw change because of an incident. These are the experiences that will refresh your faith in me and draw us closer together. What I treasure the most in our relationship is your desire for it to grow deeper!

"I can honestly say that I was never affected by the question of the success of an understanding. If I felt it was the right thing to do, I was for it regardless of the possible outcome."

Golda Meir

Words to Ponder: It is sometimes hard to know what we are called to do in certain situations. We may look at the situation from all angles, weigh the pros and cons, and pray about it, yet we still struggle to make the right decision. At such times, there comes a moment where we often experience a feeling within - a sense of calm or peace - and the answers to what we need to do become evident. Some call it listening to your heart, some the voice of God, but when we move ahead with our decision, we are at peace.

God Whispered: I created you to be my reflection to others. Never doubt my constant love and support in what you want to do with your life. I am here to give you the confidence and strength to accomplish whatever the desire of your heart is despite the consequences. I will always be with you in any situation.

"True intimacy with another human being can only be experienced when you have found true peace within yourself."

Angela L. Wozniak

Words to Ponder: Sharing our intimate thoughts and sharing our life with another helps us have a peaceful spirit, because we feel loved, confident, and whole. Whenever we open ourselves up to another, we risk getting hurt or rejected. But it is a risk worth taking to experience peace within us.

God Whispered: I want a closer relationship with you. Even though I know you, I want you to feel like you can tell me anything. Continue to come to me with your joys, sorrows, and disappointments. I want to free you of your fears and help you realize that I will always be there for you. Never doubt my love and support. Let go of your worrying. Trust in me and you will live a peaceful life.

"The ability for a group of people to do remarkable things hinges on how well those people can pull together as a team."

Simon Sinek

Words to Ponder: Learning to work as part of a team is so important. There is no "I" in team. My two campus ministry interns, Addisen Carino and Liz Akerly, are a delight to work with. They know what it means to work as a team. They were amazed as they shared their creative ideas and used their gifts to make the women's retreat and our annual Dinner Dance successful. The work they did was not only inspiring but also beneficial to all who came to the retreat and to the Dinner Dance. By working as a team, you can accomplish more than you can imagine. Often projects where people are encouraged to share creative ideas and brainstorm solutions turn out the best.

God Whispered: I am happy when you want to work as a team. I want you to live in peace and harmony. Learning how to work together, sharing your ideas and dreams can be liberating and help you to become the one I created you to be. Keep up the good work. I am so proud of you.

"The perception of what's possible is on the other side of fear!"

Leslie Zann

Words to Ponder: Fear can destroy creativity. Sometimes fear paralyzes us, and other times it drives us to do things we would normally never think of doing. To overcome fear we have to challenge ourselves to do something out of the ordinary. I remember being with a friend in Chicago who told me he was filled with all sorts of fear. As we were standing by the train, two men came up to him and took his wallet. He turned around and grabbed the man who had his wallet and yelled at him. The six foot man dropped the wallet and ran. When we got on the train, I said, "Well, you just overcame your fear. I would never in a million years try and get a wallet back from someone that big. He could have taken a gun out and killed you." He smiled and said, "Maybe I am not as fearful as I think."

God Whispered: I know sometimes you are afraid and proceed cautiously. While it is okay to act with caution, I don't want fear to control your life. Now that you have shown me that you can overcome your fear, I want you to look at other areas of your life. Continue to place your trust in me!

"It's impossible." said **Pride.**
"It's risky," said **Experience.**
'It's pointless," said **Reason.**
"Give it a try,"
Whispered the Heart.

Author Unknown

Words to Ponder: Usually our heart tells us what we are called to do. Our inner voice is powerful in directing our thoughts. It helps us to focus on what is important in our lives, and often directs us on the right path. We have the power to think and act on our thoughts. As we reflect on our ideas and what motivates us, the ideas that are planted deep within our mind frequently indicate the direction we plan to explore or take. We need to trust that God has a hand in all we do.

God Whispered: I want you to dream about the impossible, be willing to take risks, and always listen to your inner voice. I will always be there to guide you in the right direction. Trust that nothing is impossible as long as you ask me to be with you on your journey. By trusting in me you will experience joy and peace.

"Love cures people-both the ones who give it and the ones who receive it."

Karl Menninger

Words to Ponder: I know love can cure people. I have seen it happen. Mother Teresa said, *"People hunger more for love than food."* A priest was told that he probably had six months to live. Since he wanted to see all his friends before he died, he threw himself a party and invited people from all over the United States. It was a fantastic party. Everyone laughed, shared stories, and had a delightful time. Two weeks later, he went to his doctor and his doctor could not find any trace of cancer. He lived for ten more years. What a testimony to love! Let's continue to show our love to one another and see what a wonderful world we can make.

God Whispered: I love you with an everlasting love. You are mine! I created you to love and when you express your love to others, you and I are more closely connected than any other time. Always remember, love heals, brings joy and makes people happy

**"If you want to know where your heart is,
look where your mind goes when it wanders."**

Bella Mumma

Words to Ponder: This quote reminds me of the gospel *passage "For where your treasure is, there your heart will be also."* [Luke12:34] What we value most in life is where our heart goes. If you value things, then you will accumulate things. If you value family and friends, then you will spend your time with them. As we grow older, we tend to downsize the things we have collected along the way and put our energy in the people and relationships that feed our soul.

God Whispered: I delight in being in your presence. I desire that you glorify me with your entire being. Your life is a precious gift. As you direct your love toward me, I bless you abundantly with joy and peace. Lean on me. I am always there for you.

"God always has something for you: A key for every problem, a light for every shadow, a relief for every sorrow, and a plan for every tomorrow."

Author Unknown

Words to Ponder: If we turn our lives over to God and trust that God will always be there, our lives will be much happier. God seems to know our weakness and problems. We think we can do it on our own, but we need God to give us the guidance and grace to survive any situation. If we are aware of our weaknesses, we are not likely to boast about ourselves. We have within us everything we need to change ourselves into the best person we can be.

God Whispered: Rest assured that I will always be there to handle any situation. I will give you the strength and confidence needed to deal with anything. Relax and continue to trust in me.

"Beginning today, treat everyone as if you were going to be dead by midnight. Extend to them all the care, kindness, and understanding you can muster, and do it with no thought of any reward. Your life will never be the same."

Og Mandino

Words to Ponder: My parents always told us to live each day as if it were our last. Doing this certainly made a difference in how we treated each other and how we lived our lives. Yet we often think we will live forever or at least we act like it. We don't take the time to do those things we know we want to do. When someone we love dies, we suddenly realize things we should have said or what we should have done for that person. Don't wait! Reach out and do some act of kindness for another person today.

God Whispered: I want you to live each day to the fullest. Continue to be happy with the person you are and help others to rejoice along with you. Promise to be kind and faithful. Let these promises ignite your gratitude. Bask in my love for you. Know that I fill your happy heart with a love that will draw others to me. Invite me to guide you along the way.

"You can make just about anything of your life - anything you will believe or will visualize, anything you will pray for and work for. Look deeply into your mind. Amazing wonders are there."

Norman Vincent Peale

Words to Ponder: It is amazing what we can accomplish in our lives when we learn to believe in ourselves. It is incredible how our energy increases once we learn how to visualize our successes. By learning how to use the gifts and talents we have been given in a positive way, we can surpass our limitations. When we are authentic, our spirits soar and our creative spirit thrives.

God Whispered: I know what you are capable of doing. Rejoice in the gifts that you have. Look deeply into your being and discover how much more you are capable of doing. If you can visualize it, then you can do it with my grace. Turn to me when you need guidance and I will be there to help you in any situation.

"Love is a partnership of two unique people who bring out the very best in each other and who know that even though they are wonderful as individuals, they even are better together."

Barbara Cage

Words to Ponder: We all have seen what love can do to another person. Love has healed people. Love brings out the best in another and gives people courage to do things they would not necessarily do. When love is absent, people feel unimportant, alone and forgotten. To be loved by another is the deepest desire of our hearts.

God Whispered: I have created you to love each other, and when you do that you make me happy. Always remember that nothing on earth can separate you from my love. My love for you is inexhaustible. It outweighs the many problems you may have experienced. I will continue to surround you with my unfailing love. I am with you in all circumstances. My love completes you.

"The greatest challenge in life is discovering who you are. The second greatest is being happy with what you find."

Author Unknown

Words to Ponder: Discovering who we are and what we are called to do can be quite challenging, but once discovered, it is amazing how much joy and energy we receive. Finding a job or ministry where we can use our gifts, love what we do and feel like we are making a difference is part of God's plan for us. He wants us to have a happy, productive life. Reflect on the following:

Happiness
Happiness comes now and then, we cannot be sure just when.
But when it's there, enjoy each hour,
because happiness has such power,
Joy to you it will bring, even make someone else sing.
What peace of mind happiness can show,
making you and others glow,
nurture it, make it last,
forget the troubles of the past.
Never fear that it will go, for it could always grow
and then tomorrow there it will be,
for happiness can set you free.
Author Unknown

43

God Whispered: Once you discover your gifts, use them to glorify me. I have designed you to ask for my help so you can be the best person you can be. As I fill you with my love, it will overflow into the lives of others - bringing them joy and peace. It gives me great pleasure to see you happy and at peace. It is what all parents want for their children.

**"When life is sweet, say thank you and celebrate.
And when life is bitter, say thank you and grow."**

Shauna Niequist

Words to Ponder: Don't we all want to celebrate the gift of life and be happy? One way we can be happier is to cultivate an attitude of gratitude. By making a habit of acknowledging not only **what** we are grateful for but also **who** we are grateful for (and their specific traits), we will be happier because we are concentrating on what is right in our lives. Gratitude can even help us through the tough times. We can keep our troubles in perspective by remembering our many blessings and giving thanks. God wants to be with us at all times. When we turn to God, he gives us the strength we need to overcome our insecurities, pain, and sorrow.

God Whispered: I am here to celebrate with you in good times and bad. Joy is freeing. Gratitude is as contagious as joy. The more you express it, the happier you become. Look to me and remember I am with you always.

"A nation should not be judged by how it treats its highest citizens, but it's lowest ones."

Nelson Mandela

Words to Ponder: It is amazing what we witness sometimes. A priest friend, who lived very simply, had a great love for the poor and was involved in social justice issues. He was well respected by the people in town. He wanted to see how others, who did not know him, would treat him if they did not know he was a priest. He married a couple and headed off to the reception. The reception was held at a very exclusive place. He drove there in his old beat up truck with a cousin of the wedding party. The guard, at the entrance, would not even let them get out the truck. He did not even look inside. They were asked to leave and told not to bother to return for the reception. He left, parked his truck and returned. He was welcomed royally. He then introduced himself to the guard and told him what he did. The guard was shocked and apologized.

God Whispered: I want you to treat everyone with the respect and dignity they deserve. Do not judge others by how they dress or the type of car they drive. Remember you are all my children and I love you unconditionally.

"Life seldom presents us with challenges we can't meet, with obstacles we can't overcome or with problems that can't be solved. We simply have to approach each problem with a positive attitude and know that it's only a matter of persistence and time before we arrive at a solution."

George Shinn

Words to Ponder: When we cultivate a certain attitude, whether it is one of joy or sadness, indifference or selfishness, it will determine how the events of our lives affect us. We can't control the different obstacles that we encounter in our daily lives, but we are in charge of our attitudes. When we have a positive attitude, most of the time positive experiences happen. We attract people like ourselves. If you are a positive person, then positive and happy people will be drawn to you. Only you can change your attitude. Are you willing to take charge of your attitude and make a positive difference?

God Whispered: Invite me into your situation and let me help you. I know the desires of your heart. You can't control people, only things. Trust me; there is a solution even if you can't see it at this time.

"As long as you as an individual... can convince yourself that in order to move forward as best you can you have to be optimistic, you can be described as 'one of the faithful,' one of those people who can say, 'Well, look, something's going to happen! Let's just keep trying. Let's not give up.'"

Tom Hanks

Words to Ponder: As children, we were encouraged not to give up on anything we wanted in life. If we failed, our parents told us to keep trying. Is there something that you want badly enough that you will keep trying? If you know in your heart that it is good for you, continue to pursue it. Always choose what is good, honest and right, only then will you will experience a sense of peace and joy.

God Whispered: I created you to go after what you desire in your heart. I don't want you to give up those things you are passionate about. Call on me and I will be there to help you.

**"...a person who is comfortable gossiping <u>to you</u> is,
I promise, perfectly comfortable gossiping <u>about you.</u>
Love is the answer here: love someone enough to believe
that everything you hear is not true.
Love someone enough to assume good motives until
they personally prove otherwise to you."**

Author Unknown

Words to Ponder: Love is the answer to all our problems. My dad had this saying, *"If you can't tell the world she's a good little girl, then don't say anything at all."* I recall one evening at the dinner table someone's name came up. All seven of us knew things about this person that were not good. In fact, this person did mean and hurtful things to people, but was so nice around my dad. Every one of us remained silent. My dad looked at all of us and said, *"What's the matter?"* We looked at each other and then said, *"Remember Dad, what you taught us, 'If you can't tell the world she's a good little girl, then don't say anything at all.'"* He shook his head and smiled saying, "Well, I guess you at least remember what I taught you!" We changed the conversation and finished our meal. We all need to try and avoid situations that will lead to gossip. Gossip is horrible because of the damage it does to the persons involved. I remember seeing this poem when I was a child. It hung in the rectory of Msgr. Henige who lived in Pewamo, Michigan.

Nobody's Friend

My name is Gossip.

I have no respect for justice.

I maim without killing.

I break hearts and ruin lives.

I am cunning and malicious and gather strength with age.

The more I am quoted the more I am believed.

My victims are helpless.

They cannot protect themselves against me because
            I have no name and no face.

To track me down is impossible.

The harder you try, the more elusive I become.

I am nobody's friend.

Once I tarnish a reputation, it is never the same.

I topple governments and wreck marriages.

I ruin careers and cause sleepless nights, heartaches, and indigestion.

I make innocent people cry in their pillows.

Even my name hisses.

I am called Gossip.

I make headlines and headaches.

Before you repeat a story, ask yourself:

Is it true?

Is it harmless?

Is it necessary?

If it isn't, don't repeat it.   Author Unknown

God Whispered: I created you to love each other. I am calling you to live in a spirit of love and kindness. Let your thoughts and words be flavored with gratitude, kindness, and honesty. It doesn't matter what others say or do, you are to walk with me allowing me to help you spread joy. Because you are mine, I want to bless you with the love that sees the good others. I will bless you with radiant peace and turn your life into something beautiful!

"To be near something beautiful or precious, but to be unable to experience it is the subtlest possible form of torture."

Robert Johnson

Words to Ponder: How often do we miss those things that are right in front of us? This quote reminds me of a friend who lives in California. She invited me for a visit to see her new home, and the beautiful view she had of the ocean. The day I arrived it was so foggy that I had trouble finding her home. The drive up the mountain was scary. I could not see where I was going. I think she was more upset than I was when I finally arrived and couldn't see her beautiful view of the ocean. Three days later the fog lifted, and I was able to rejoice with her and enjoy the beautiful view.

God Whispered: I want you to experience and enjoy the beauty of my creation. Sometimes you may have to be patient, but the wait will be worth it.

"Peace is the result of retraining your mind to process life as it is, rather than as you think it should be."

Wayne W. Dyer

Words to Ponder: I believe that peace is something that comes from within. It is accepting life as it is and moving forward. I don't think there is only one way to be at peace. Each of us is different and we all look at life through different lenses. When we sit silently in the presence of God and center ourselves, we become more peaceful. Silence is the beginning of peace.

God Whispered: Sit silently in my presence and let me flood you with my graces. I want you to trust in me, and know that I will always be there for you. I will supply all your needs, and give you the desires of your heart. Remember peace is a supernatural gift that comes from me.

"Stop letting people who do so little for you control so much of your mind, feelings and emotions."

Will Smith

Words to Ponder: Why do we give power to people who are so controlling? Controlling individuals desire to have power over us because it makes them feel important. Instead we need to surround ourselves with people we trust, people who accept us, encourage us and bring out the best in us. Take time today to pray for all those in your life.

God Whispered: I want you to get to know me more intimately. I have been initiating a closer relationship with you. When you depend on me and ask for guidance and strength, I will be there. Try not to give people more power than they deserve. Some are insecure and have a need to feel important. Rely on my continual love for you and try not to doubt that I am going to be there for you. You are with me always.

"There comes a time in your life when you walk away from all the drama and people who create it.
You surround yourself with people who make you laugh.
Forget the bad, and focus on the good.
Love the people who treat you right, pray for the ones who don't.
Life is too short to be anything but happy.
Falling down is a part of life, getting back up is living."

José N. Harris

Words to Ponder: We all want to surround ourselves with people who lift our spirits. We need to surround ourselves with positive people. We need to choose those people who encourage, support, and are there for us no matter what.

God Whispered: Know that I will never leave you. I committed to you the day you were born. I am here for the long haul. I will always be here to lift your spirits and calm your confused mind. I will help you focus on the good you do and the people who treat you with love and respect.

**"It makes no difference what you look like on the outside
if you don't love yourself on the inside."**

Anna Pereira

Words to Ponder: Society today seems to place great value on our physical appearance. As a result of this preoccupation, people have all sorts of plastic surgery, face lifts, tummy tucks – hoping that they will feel better about themselves. Unfortunately, many still don't feel better because happiness is an inside job. It is who we are on the inside and how we treat others that matters. If we want to learn how to love ourselves on the inside, we begin by living our life for others, being honest and trustworthy in our relationships, and living life with integrity. Our physical bodies are only temporary, we need to cultivate what is lasting – the beauty and love in our souls.

God Whispered: You always look beautiful to me. I know your soul. Work on being true to the person I called you to be. That makes me happy. Continue to be a person of integrity. Live a life worthy of your calling. Believe in my love for you.

**"Don't be too hard on yourself.
There are plenty of people willing to do that for you.
Love yourself and be proud of everything that you do.
Even mistakes mean you're trying."**

Susan Gale

Words to Ponder: I have been told that this is one thing I am guilty of: being too hard on myself. As a child, my mom said, "I am so glad that God is the one who will judge you in the end, because you expect more of yourself than anyone." It is okay to have high expectations, but we must also realize that we will make mistakes; what is important is learning from our mistakes and becoming the person God intended us to be.

God Whispered: I know you and understand you completely. You may stumble and fall all the way to the kingdom, but each time you lift yourself up, you make me happy. I am always here to help you. I am the one who understands you better than anyone and loves you without question. Trust in me and you will live a more peaceful and happy life.

"Give the ones you love wings to fly, roots to come back and reasons to stay."

Dalai Lama

Words to Ponder: My parents loved all seven of us the way we needed to be loved. Not only did they give us wings to fly, but they also gave us guidelines to live by. They planted deep within our soul's reasons for us to come back or stay. When we look back at our lives, many of us realize the gift our family and faith have been. We are drawn back to the source who gave us life!

God Whispered: My love for you is unbreakable. I will never curtail your freedom or stop you from doing what you feel called to do. Remember, I gave you free will and I respect that. I want you to use it wisely. No matter how far away you may fly from me, I will always welcome you back. I will even run to meet you half way. I see the desires of your heart, and I am pleased that you want to return to your source of love and faithfulness.

**"I think it's very healthy to spend time alone.
You need to know how to be alone and not be defined
by another person."**

Oscar Wilde

Words to Ponder: Anyone who knows me knows that I am an extrovert. However, I still need my quiet time with God to collect my thoughts and listen to where God is leading me. It is in the silence that we hear God's voice. The times we are aware of him, we don't feel alone or lost. At times, we all find ourselves unaware of God's presence and then feel lonely.

God Whispered: I am always there for you, but you may not always be conscious of my presence. Sometimes I think you may be afraid of being alone. Remember I am in your heart and in your mind, and your desire to be alone will be filled with my love and peace. Your feelings of loneliness speak of your need to come to me. I am the only one who can fill your emptiness. Trust in me and you will find peace.

**"Being honest may not get you a lot of friends
but it'll always get you the right ones."**

John Lennon

Words to Ponder: "Honesty is the best policy," was my dad's favorite saying. Our true friends are those we can be perfectly honest with, and we know that they will not judge us because of our honesty. We need friends who speak the truth, especially those who speak the truth with kindness. We may have to encourage new friends to tell us the truth, rather than what they think we want to hear, as they may be trying to spare our feelings. Flattery can be superficial and we can sense when it is not real.

God Whispered: I want you to trust me enough to be totally yourself. I bring out the best in you when you are true to yourself. I will give you the courage to be honest in any situation. I respect and love you, therefore I will never leave you. Just call out my name and I will give you the strength needed to accomplish any task. I will give you friends who will support you and affirm you.

"The only people with whom you should try to get even are those who have helped you."

John E. Southard

Words to Ponder: At one time or another, each of us has needed help. Perhaps a job was lost or a loved one died. Your friends rallied around you, giving you comfort and much needed support. Now it is our turn, to not only remember those who helped us, but to reach out and help those in need. When we are able to help others, we feel good. We experience a sense of gratification and peacefulness. Of course, the perfect challenge is to do something for someone who can't pay us back. It's amazing what that will do to our self-esteem.

God Whispered: I created people to love and help one another. It pleases me when they care for each other. Give voice to what you desire in your heart. I am pleased when you give generously from your want, not your abundance.

"Never confuse people who are always around you, with people who are always there for you."

Gee Linder

Words to Ponder: We learn quickly who our real friends are when there is a need. People may hang around us and act like they are a friend, but when something comes up and we need them, they are not there. At that point, we question their friendship. True friends do everything in their power to be there for us when we need them and even when we don't. Let's strive to be the type of friend who will be there for others, especially when they are suffering or need someone.

God Whispered: I am there for you when you need me. Turn to me, know that I am there. I have written your name on my heart and it can't be erased.

**"If you want to be successful, you must respect one rule:
NEVER LIE TO YOURSELF."**

Paulo Coelho

Words to Ponder: What do we accomplish by lying to ourselves? While we may want to be successful, we will never find peace or happiness as long as we continue to lie to ourselves. We will only experience a deep sense of peace when we are willing to face ourselves honestly. That peace will replace any fear or anxiety that we have.

God Whispered: I know you want to be successful, but true success is being true to yourself. I watch the transformation that takes place in you every day. As you respond positively to me in this adventure, I will help you become more fully the person I designed you to be: a person who is full of joy, peace, and love.

**"May the stars carry your sadness away,
May the flowers fill your heart with beauty,
May hope forever wipe away your tears,
And, above all, may silence make you strong."**

Chief Dan George

Words to Ponder: We all need silence in our lives. It is when we are silent that we become aware of all we have, what we need to change and what we need to develop. Silence helps us reflect more on our faith life, calls us to spend more time in prayer and helps us to deepen our relationship with God.

God Whispered: I can take your sadness away, fill your beautiful heart with love and with compassion. I can remove any pain that has caused you tears, and help you to be strong in your commitment to me. All you have to do is ask. I will be there. It brings joy to me when you are consistently seeking me. Your thoughts and requests have a powerful influence on your well-being. I am always here to help you live a happy and healthy life. Remain open to me and I will fill your heart with joy and take your sadness away.

"One of the hardest decisions you'll ever face in life is choosing whether to walk away or try harder."

Ziad K. Abdelnour

Words to Ponder: It is so easy to walk away from a situation that may be difficult. The hardest decision is to face the challenge. We always learn something from facing a difficult situation. The attitude we have when we enter into a situation cannot only change the outcome, but also help us have the confidence we need to face future situations. By inviting God to guide us and be part of the situation, we stay in tune with the spiritual aspect and can achieve more harmonious outcomes.

God Whispered: I want you to be at peace. I want you to count on me to be there with you every step of the way. I gaze at you with so much love and I love you regardless of how well you perform. My love for you is unwavering. Turn to me, know that I am always there, and will guide you every step along the way.

"It's better to walk alone than with a crowd going in the wrong direction."

Diane Grant

Words to Ponder: I was brought up to stand up for what I knew was right rather than always following the crowd. I still remember my dad's words: "You may stand alone, but it's better to stand alone and be at peace than not be true to yourself and be unhappy." Sometimes this is difficult to do when you are young and want to be a part of a crowd, but in the end, you really don't stand alone. Your true friends want to be with someone going in the right direction.

God Whispered: I am proud of you when you stand up for what is right. I am always with you. I will give you the confidence and strength to face whatever comes your way. Never be afraid to ask for my help. I am always there for you.

**"God speaks in the silence of the heart.
Listening is the beginning of prayer."**

Mother Teresa

Words to Ponder: Prayer has been described as having a conversation with God. We are encouraged to talk to God, as we would a good friend about our concerns and how we can become a better person. We need to listen to God, whether it is through the scriptures, meditation, contemplation, or prayer. We lead such busy lives, yet it seems more and more of us are spending time going to Adoration and practicing meditation, listening to what God has to say. This time allows our inner voices to help us follow the right path.

God Whispered: I love it when you listen to me. I will always guide you in the direction that you need to go in order to be the person I intend you to become. Know you can count on me. The more you realize how much I love you, the more you will be willing to listen.

"Never laugh at or judge someone because you never know, someday you might find yourself in the same situation."

Brigitte Nicole

Words to Ponder: A brother refused to go to his sister's wedding because she was marrying someone of a different faith. While it hurt his sister, she forgave him because she knew he loved her, but didn't approve of what she did. A few years later, her brother's son got married within a different faith. This same sister, and the rest of the family, came to the wedding to support him because he was their brother even though they didn't support the idea of his son's marriage outside of the church. Sometimes the loving thing to do means swallowing our pride and doing things we never dreamed.

God Whispered: I know you may not always approve of what people do but you are called to love them. The more you love one another, the deeper your relationship with me will grow. You may not always like what people do, but you are called to love others, not judge them.

"NEVER GIVE UP; never lose hope.
Always have faith, it allows you to cope.
Trying times will pass as they always do.
Just have patience; your dreams will come true.
So put on a smile, you will live through your pain.
Know it will pass, and strength you will gain."

Bel Claveria Carig Martinez

Words to Ponder: We are part of the now generation. We desire things to happen NOW. We want instant gratification and often lack patience. Yet having said this, we must never give up on our dreams. At times, we may lack the wisdom and patience to deal with things that challenge us, or we may lack confidence to move forward. Remember to turn to God and ask him to help you in times like this. He will give you the strength to believe in yourself and help you cope with things that come your way.

God Whispered: I never want you to give up hope. Call on me no matter how hopeless your situation may seem or how impatient you are in wanting something to happen. I am there to help you and assure you that all things are possible when you put me first in your life.

"When the Japanese mend broken objects, they aggrandize the damage by filling the cracks with gold. They believe that when something's suffered damage and has a history it becomes more beautiful."

Barbara Bloom

Words to Ponder: In the movie *Joshua*, a young woman lost her husband in a terrible accident. Her life was shattered. In her anger, she threw down a beautiful glass vase in front of Joshua, symbolizing what a mess her life was. It shattered into thousands of pieces. Later, Joshua took the broken pieces and made a beautiful glass heart. When he presented it to the young woman days later, she recognized the glass and was deeply touched. What a perfect reminder that from our brokenness God can create something beautiful.

God Whispered: It is your inner beauty that I value. I know the brokenness in your life, and I will always take it and make something better. It is when you are hurting that you come to me. You grow from each experience. I am here for you and will continue to be there for you in times of trouble.

"You may have made a lot of wrong choices, but you've also made a lot of choices that were right. Focus on your good qualities. Focus on your victories. Get off the treadmill of guilt."

Joel Osteen

Words to Ponder: Wouldn't it be great if we could eliminate the guilt we experience? When we make a mistake, we punish ourselves. When we feel we can't measure up to what others say, we have a tendency to get down on ourselves. While it is important to learn from our mistakes and make amends, it is not healthy to continue to carry the guilt around. We need to learn how to move on, focus on the good things we do and the positive things that are happening.

God Whispered: I want you to make choices that will be good for you and bring you happiness. Happiness comes from living the right kind of life. It is a form of freedom. Each time you choose something good for yourself, peacefulness and joy fill your soul. Whenever you find yourself worrying, turn to me and I will show you the way that will lead you on a happy and peaceful journey.

"Anytime you start a sentence with, 'I am,' you are creating what you are and what you want to be. When you choose to say, 'I am happy, I am kind, I am perfect,' you help the light of God inside you grow and shine."

Dr. Wayne Dyer

Words to Ponder: We will experience happiness when we begin to take time to listen to our inner selves. When we are happy, we have a tendency to be kind and thoughtful. We have often heard the statement: "Become perfect as our heavenly father is perfect." This doesn't mean we will never make a mistake; rather that we are called to love others like God loves us, a perfect love.

God Whispered: I want you to shine from within, and spread my love and joy to all those you meet. Joy is infectious. When you are around someone who is joyful, it makes you want to be happy. I will fill you with my joy, so that your joy will touch others and help heal them.

"Having a soft heart in a cruel world is courage, not weakness."

Katherine Henson

Words to Ponder: My dad had such a soft heart. He loved people. I saw how compassionate and sensitive he was to others. I remember the first time I saw him cry I was deeply touched. I thought he was courageous. I never considered him weak. My dad told my brothers that a man shows his strength by being kind, gentle, caring, forgiving, honest, and faithful.

God Whispered: I created you all to have gentle hearts. I want your hearts to be open and to show love to those who are hurting. It is not a sign of weakness; it is a sign of strength and courage. A wave of peacefulness will come over you when you have accomplished this.

"Once you begin to acknowledge random acts of kindness... both the ones you have received and the ones you have given... you can no longer believe that what you do does not matter.
Too often we underestimate the power of a touch, a smile, a kind word, a listening ear, an honest compliment, or the smallest act of caring... all of which have the potential to turn a life around..."

Leo Buscaglia

Words to Ponder: I just finished watching the movie, "Pay it Forward," for the third time. This movie shows how one random act of kindness changed peoples' lives. The students were asked by their social studies teacher to come up with one idea that would improve the world. One young boy decided that if he could do three good deeds for others, they, in turn, could "pay it forward" and a positive chain reaction would occur. The initial recipients were: his badly scarred teacher, a drug addict, and a classmate who was continually bullied by his peers. It was amazing how lives were changed just from one person being kind and thoughtful.

God Whispered: Each time you show kindness to another, you will not only change one life, but your life will change as well. I want you to make a difference in this world. I created you to love and share that love with others. Please stay in constant communication with me. I will guide you as you move forward, to do things that I have placed in your heart. Your trust in me will deepen. You will do things you never imagined.

"You are so brave and quiet I forget you are suffering."

Ernest Hemingway

Words to Ponder: I remember when my mom was diagnosed with bone cancer. My family had no idea as she never complained. We realized something wasn't right when she asked us not to hug her so hard. When she fell and broke her hip, the doctor decided to run some tests. We were shocked when they told us that she had had bone cancer for over a year. They gave her two and a half weeks to two months. She suffered silently and was so brave. She didn't want us to worry about her. My mom, a woman of prayer who always had her holy hour every day, was always an inspiration to me not only by the way she lived but also how she suffered silently!

God Whispered: Allow my healing rays to lesson your suffering and heal you. Whenever you are suffering, you tend to blame me and want me to intercede. I allow you to suffer so that you can understand more of what I went through for you. When you share in my suffering, you also share in my glory and love. Don't worry. I will give you the grace and strength you will need to deal with any problem.

"One of the most courageous decisions you'll ever make is to finally let go of what is hurting your heart and soul."

Brigitte Nicole

Words to Ponder: In counseling, I find that so many people find it hard to let go of the one person who is hurting them the most. It seems they lack the self-confidence they need to do better and become a better person until they learn to trust their instincts. Once they find the courage and choose what is best for them, it is amazing how full of life they become. They begin to see their worth and value what God has created.

God Whispered: My presence is always with you. I will give you the grace and strength you need to choose a better life for yourself. I will help you learn to turn to me in those times when you are confused or hurting. You must trust my love for you. I want your heart happy and I want you to be at peace.

**"Success is not final, failure is not fatal: it is the courage
to continue that counts."**

Winston Churchill

Words to Ponder: It takes a lot of courage to continue moving forward when we haven't been successful utilizing our skills and gifts. We all want to do well in whatever we try. Through our failures we learn not only humility, but also how to be more sympathetic towards others who have failed. Once we have the courage to move forward, without looking back, we can begin again and be at peace regardless of the outcome.

God Whispered: You may not always be successful at everything you attempt. You learn from every experience. I know you turn to me in desperation when things don't go as planned. Know that I am always there for you and I will give you the courage and peace needed to continue when all seems hopeless.

"If your actions inspire others to dream more, learn more, do more, and become more, you are a leader."

John Quincy Adams

Words to Ponder: When I first started campus ministry, Fr. John Grathwohl, the pastor, gave me the freedom to dream, create, learn, and he challenged me to become "more." When a person believes in you, trusts you, and gives you the freedom to become all that you are called to be, it is amazing what you can become! Fr. Joseph Girzone also did that for me when I became the co-director of the Joshua Foundation. I accomplished things while working with him that I never dreamed I could do, including writing books. Last but not least, Fr. Mark Inglot also gave me the freedom to create and make St. John Student Center a home away from home for the students. I will forever be grateful to these priests.

God Whispered: I have called you to places where I knew you would develop into the person I intended you to become. I know how much you enjoy your freedom. When you are free, you are more creative and you draw yourself closer to me. Our relationship is so much deeper because of it. Just continue to trust in me and you will be amazed at what can happen.

**"Happiness comes from spiritual wealth, not material wealth.
Happiness is always a by-product, never a product.
Happiness comes from giving, not getting.
If we pursue happiness for ourselves, it will always elude us.
If we try hard to bring happiness to others,
we cannot stop it from coming to us also."**

Rev. Robert H. Schuller

Words to Ponder: Happiness is within my power. It is reflected in my attitude about life and how I respond to what happens to me. Things don't make us happy: people do, experiences do, and situations can. We will find happiness when we focus more on the needs of others and less on our own personal problems. The more we give of ourselves, the happier we will become. We also can find happiness when we are able to become quiet and listen to our inner voice.

God Whispered: There is nothing I want more for you than for you to be happy. The more you give to others, the happier you become. Trust in me. I know what is good for you. I will give you a new heart. As you consistently stay open, you will see the plans I have for you. Plans for you to become more than you ever dreamed!

"It's not integrity if it doesn't cost you something."

Henry Cloud

Words to Ponder: Our parents raised us to have integrity. They explained that a person who exhibits the values of honesty and truthfulness also needs to be approachable and dependable; you can always rely on their word. Maintaining our integrity, in our world today, isn't easy as it means we may be called to stand up for what we believe even if it costs us.

God Whispered: I created you to be honest and trustworthy. When you are living these values you make me happy. I know you trust me, however, at times, you start to doubt especially if things don't run as smoothly as you would like. Trust that I will straighten out the path you are on. Allow me to work with your heart. I will guide you and your walk with me will be a peaceful one.

"We need leaders who can unite us and ignite us."

Jim Kayes and Barry Posne

Words to Ponder: As a junior high teacher, I always taught my students to be a "leader for good." Good leaders challenge us not only to do our best, but also to continue learning and applying our new skills. They inspire us by being good role models. They encourage us. They mentor us and lead by example. They model integrity and are passionate about their beliefs and values. Once we have had the privilege of working with a good leader, we never want to settle for mediocrity.

God Whispered: I created you to inspire and encourage others. That is what Jesus did throughout his life. No one ever walked away from my son without feeling better about themselves. This is what I want from you. I want you to bring out the best in others and encourage them. You can always count on my love and support.

**Our most important work in this life is
to prepare ourselves for the next one."**

Fr. John McCloskey

Words to Ponder: As we prepare ourselves for the future, we have to remember that if we are open to the divine and have faith, we will want to change and grow. Faith is something that grows inside us if we continue to nurture it. It does not grow unattended. Marty Haugen sings a song: "We Walk By Faith and Not By Sight." It reminds us to be aware of God's continual love for us no matter what.

God Whispered: I want you to turn to me. Remember I am with you always. Your love for me will increase. I will never leave you. I will guide you to places you never dreamed of and I will be with you every step of the way. Your spirit will be open as long as we stay in constant communication. I know the desires of your heart and I am committed to you.

**"Example is not the main thing in influencing others.
It is the only thing."**

Albert Schweitzer

Words to Ponder: I often watched how my parents treated each other when I was growing up. They treated each other with love, kindness, and respect. "More is caught than ever taught," was a well-known expression used by many parents when I was young. If our actions do not match our words, then they are useless. Children learn so much from watching adults including: the language we use, the comments we make, how we deal with others and treat teachers, employees, friends, and other family members. We all have to remember the example we set. What we believe in our hearts must be displayed in how we live our lives.

God Whispered: I want you to be a reflection of me in how you treat others. Always show others love and kindness and continue to be positive and sincere. Remember to treasure my teachings in your heart for they will bring you peace and contentment.

"To those I may have wronged, I ask forgiveness.
To those I may have helped, I wish I did more.
To those I neglected to help, I ask for your understanding.
To those who helped me, I sincerely thank you so much."

Author Unknown

Words to Ponder: I don't think we intentionally want to hurt someone or choose not to respond to a person in need. But when that does happen, we need to ask for forgiveness. We can probably all remember a time when we were in need, and how grateful we were to all those who helped us. One way we can express our gratitude is by paying it forward. When we practice gratitude, we become more aware of those who give without counting the cost.

God Whispered: I want you to ask for forgiveness when you hurt someone. I am pleased when you give to those in need, and show appreciation for those who go out of their way to help you or others. By learning to be grateful, you will change your attitude about life, soften your heart, and make yourself more loveable.

"Although I am an atheist and have no religion, our only hope for peace in this world is by following the philosophy and way of life of Jesus. His life is relevant to all of us, no matter what our beliefs. His teachings make sense in our troubled world."

President of an African Country
speaking to other African Leaders

Words to Ponder: I remember a young man I met at Western Michigan University while walking to my office on campus. It was my first year as a campus minister, and I was so excited and happy to be doing this work. He came up to me and asked me, "What makes you happy and gives you peace?"

At first I was shocked, then I responded, "What makes me happy is using the gifts I have been given, and doing things that give me life and a sense of fulfillment." I shared that I worked at this church and was a campus minister. I invited him to come and check it out.

He said, "I am an atheist and don't believe in that stuff."

I replied, "I didn't tell you to believe in the things that I believe in. I am just sharing with you what gives me peace. I would love to have you come just once to Mass and see for yourself."

He came that Sunday and the following three Sundays. I finally stopped him and asked, "What makes you keep coming here?"

He said, "All I can say is that I feel better after I leave here and I like what the guy up there has to say."

I said, "That is good enough for me."

That young man came to Mass faithfully every Sunday for three years. He brought his parents to the Graduation Mass. They were shocked that he attended Mass. I told them how proud I was of their son who had been coming faithfully for three years even though he told me he was an atheist. They just smiled. We had a wonderful conversation and they left happy and pleased. What a sacramental moment!

God Whispered: My teachings make sense. They are about loving, forgiving, and caring for others. They are the way to peace and happiness. I am proud of the work that has been accomplished by those who trust me and want to model their life after mine.

"What you get by achieving your goals is not as important as what you become by achieving your goals."

Henry David Thoreau

Words to Ponder: It is a well-known fact that when you affirm someone for something they have done, they often become better. People who have been affirmed seem to accomplish more because someone believed in them. Receiving praise for what you have accomplished increases confidence, helps build self-esteem, and makes goals more attainable.

God Whispered: Let me help you accomplish the goals you have set for yourself. As you learn to trust me, you stop listening to your thoughts and worrying about everything. Remember that I know what happens to you every second. I never take my eyes off you. As you draw on me for strength and direction, I will lead you. You will achieve great things.

"Trust is built on telling the truth, not telling people what they want to hear."

Simon Sinek

Words to Ponder: Trust is one of the most important values needed in order to have a lasting relationship. If you can't trust a person, how can you commit your life to them? A friendship will not last if trust is not one of the main values. Relationships are built on trust and honesty. When people are honest, they may tell you things, with kindness, that you may not want to hear, but if it is the truth, then your friendship will grow into something beautiful for God.

God Whispered: Continue to place your trust in me. I am always here for you in good times and bad, I will never leave you. Never doubt my love for you. My love for you never runs out. I am committed to you for eternity.

"You have succeeded in life when all you really want is only what you really need."

Vernon Howard

Words to Ponder: Whenever my friends and I would go shopping, we would ask ourselves, "Is this a want or a need?" The majority of the time they were things we wanted, not things we needed. As children, we tend to want lots of "stuff." As we get older, we realize that having all that "stuff" does not fill the need that every human heart longs for. We may decide to downsize, get rid of, or donate what we don't use and concentrate on what we really need. What we all need is to be loved and to love!

God Whispered: I am the only one who can fill the deepest longing in your heart. You may want things but what I give you will last and sustain you. I know you will always desire more love from others and especially more of my healing love.

"Patience is the ballast of the soul that will keep it from rolling and tumbling in the greatest storms."

Charles Hopkins

Words to Ponder: We all have heard that "Patience is a virtue." Abraham is a perfect example of patience in the Old Testament. He and his wife Sara didn't have their first child until he was 100. He waited 25 years for God to send him his son Isaac. Now that is patience! Patience is a learned trait and is not always easy. How do you act when you are rushing to get to the airport for your flight, waiting in the doctor's office, or in a long line at a grocery store? You know you are learning patience when you can be in those types of situations and not take your frustrations out on others.

God Whispered: Let me remind you that I am in control and I know what your needs are before you ask. Seek my peace first and then ask for patience. I will give you the strength you need. Do not worry. I am here to help you when you call upon me. My word will refresh you and give you the comfort and peace you desire.

"People take different roads seeking fulfillment and happiness. Just because they're not on your road doesn't mean they've gotten lost."

Dalai Lama

Words to Ponder: We all struggle, at times, to find fulfillment and happiness. We may try several different jobs before we discover what we are meant to do and who we are meant to be. No two people are alike or have the same priorities. What worked for our parents, or even our siblings, may not work for us. Whenever you are struggling, spend some time with God and seek his guidance along the way. He will help you discover the path you are to follow.

God Whispered: Come to me in your emptiness. You are not lost, you are still searching. I will help you discover the desire of your heart. The closer you are to me, the less lost you will feel. You may experience detours along the way. When that happens, turn to me and I will guide you in the right direction. I will never abandon you as long as you call upon me for help and guidance.

"Routine and predictable days are the breeding grounds for complacency."

Wayde Goodall

Words to Ponder: Most of us are creatures of habit and tend to follow certain routines. Have you ever noticed that you take the same way to work (school, town) and back every day? After a while, we get so comfortable with that route that we don't pay as close attention as we should. We get complacent. Sometimes, changing our routine can have great results. For example, a man took an alternative route to visit friends. He went through a small town, got gas, and noticed they had posted a job that was exactly what he was looking for. He applied and accepted the position. He was so excited about his new job. It was everything he had dreamed of doing. Sometimes when we shake things up and change our routine, the results can be exactly what we needed.

God Whispered: Doing things differently can be exciting and fulfilling. Take time to enjoy new things, go new places, and live your life to the fullest. When you are happy and doing what you love, I rejoice along with you.

**"You never know when a moment and a
few sincere words can have an impact on a life."**

Zig Ziglar

Words to Ponder: We may not realize how a few words or a simple act of kindness can impact others, until we have experienced how life can change in one split second of time. Once that happens to us, we learn to choose our words wisely, to use words that inspire, give hope, and bring about peace. Let your words be life giving and bring happiness into a person's life.

God Whispered: I created you to be a life giver. Your thoughtfulness and kindness is what I admire the most. You reflect me when you show love and give hope to another. My desire is for you to have a positive impact on the people you meet. They need my support, guidance, and love.

"Happiness isn't about getting what you want all the time; it's about loving what you have."

Asher Roth

Words to Ponder: We all deserve happiness. When we touch the soul of another, in a positive way, we tap the well of happiness that is within each one of us. True happiness isn't about things; it is about having great relationships with others. It is about being content with what we have and at peace where we are headed.

God Whispered: My desire is always to see you happy and at peace. When you love others and are happy then I am very pleased. Continue to walk with me and know that you are loved unconditionally. Put your trust in me. I will take care of your needs.

**"For if you do not know what hurts me,
how can you truly love me?"**

Hasidic story from Madeleine L'Engle's
"Walking on Water"

Words to Ponder: There is a saying, "You always hurt the one you love." I never quite understood what that meant until I got older. When we love someone, we usually know a lot about them. We know their strengths and weaknesses, their virtues and faults, and what areas they are sensitive about. We know exactly what buttons to push that will hurt them when we are angry or upset. A wise person learns not to lash out in ways that can cause lasting damage to a relationship, and when to apologize for saying hurtful things when in a bad mood.

God Whispered: We all have been hurt by someone. I admire the fact that you continue on and try not to lash out at others. I am pleased that you would rather walk away than say something you may be sorry for. When you are angry or hurt, come to me. I will listen and help you choose what to do, what will be best for you.

"Friendship is born at that moment when one person says to another, What! You too? I thought I was the only one!"

C. S. Lewis

Words to Ponder: When two people discover that they have a lot in common, they bond quickly. Perhaps they find that they come from similar backgrounds, share the same interests, or have the same values and beliefs. We may feel drawn to others who share our values and beliefs and find that what we have in common becomes the foundation of a lasting friendship.

God Whispered: I am happy you have friends who love and support you. I want you to spend time with friends you can share your feelings with. Remember I also care about you and want you to stay connected to me. Stay close to me, I will give you strength.

"The deepest principle in human nature is the craving to be appreciated."

William James

Words to Ponder: The desire of every human heart is to be loved and appreciated. When we feel appreciated, we want to give more. Sometimes we take one another for granted. We forget to let the people we interact with know how much we appreciate the work they do, or thank them for the kindness they have shown us. By thanking others and acknowledging their contributions and hard work, we help bring out the best in people.

God Whispered: I want you to treat others the way you want to be treated. Show them your kindness, respect and appreciation. As you go through each day, turn to me and trust that I will provide what you need.

"You cannot have a positive life and a negative mind."

Joyce Meyer

Words to Ponder: Our attitude affects the outcome of any situation. Positive thinking helps us deal with stress and can even improve our health. It is believed that having a positive outlook enables us to cope better in stressful situations. In recent years, a number of articles have been written on how to replace negative thinking with "positive self-talk." By practicing positive self-talk, and learning to believe in ourselves, we have the power to change our lives for the better.

God Whispered: I believe in you and I want you to have a positive, peaceful life. I know your thoughts. Sometimes you are too hard on yourself. Spend time with me and I will help you in your thoughts so they become positive and life-giving.

"Weigh the true advantages of forgiveness and resentment to the heart. Then choose."

Jack Kornfield

Words to Ponder: Forgiveness is an ongoing process. Part of that process is the realization that we can forgive someone, yet still not approve of what they have done. We are, however, at a point where we leave judgment up to God. Forgiving ourselves is probably the hardest thing we will have to learn how to do, but it is the only way that we will experience peace of mind.

God Whispered: I know that forgiveness is difficult. I had to forgive those who killed my son. Ask me to help you let go of any anger or resentment you may feel, as it hurts you more than anyone else. I will help you learn to let go and forgive, as I want you to experience inner peace.

**"You didn't use all your strength,
you didn't ask me to help."**

David J. Wolpe

Words to Ponder: Often we get so busy doing things that we forget to call upon God to help us. Or perhaps, we decide that we don't want to bother God with the "small things" we feel we can handle. Then we get exhausted, and start complaining that we don't have any strength left to accomplish the remaining tasks. I have found that our days go better when we remember to start our day by asking God for his help, strength, and guidance.

God Whispered: Let's take one day at a time. Turn to me and stay close to me. I am always here, just waiting for you to ask for my help. I do not push myself on you. I will be your strength and guide. Do not be afraid to call upon me.

"Make a gift of your life and lift all...by being kind, considerate, forgiving, and compassionate at all times, in all places, and under all conditions, with everyone as well as yourself. This is the greatest gift anyone can give."

David R. Hawkins

Words to Ponder: Life is a gift and what we give to others comes back to us in one form or another. We will be amazed at how people respond when we show them kindness, consideration and compassion. My experience has been that when we treat others this way, it returns back like a boomerang. Take a moment and try to remember all the kind things people have done for you. Make sure you thank them when you see them or perhaps even write them a note, and then think about what acts of kindness you can do for others today.

God Whispered: I created you to always be considerate and kind. I want you to be willing to forgive others and show compassion. When you live these qualities, you become a reflection of me. Remember kindness can soften the heart of those who are angry and heal broken hearts.

"My life is so beautiful that I won't agree to go back into my past even if you pay me well."

Sandra Bullock

Words to Ponder: I have always tried to live my life to the fullest and have very few regrets. I remember when my mom was dying. Some friends asked me if I had any regrets about how I treated her. I know that I loved my mom the best I could and every day I spent with her was beautiful. She taught me so much about life and love. She was my best friend, my prayer partner and my counselor. When she died, it felt like there was a hole in my heart for a long time; but I also knew that I did all the things I wanted to do for her while she was alive.

God Whispered: I never want you to live with regrets. Live each day as if it was your last. When you think you should do something for someone, do it, don't put it off. You have been placed on this earth to love and bring out the best in others. I am here for you. I love you and will never let you down.

"A true friend sympathizes freely, advises justly, assists readily, adventures boldly, takes all patiently, defends courageously, and continues a friend unchangeably."

William Penn

Words to Ponder: When you find a friend who can have all these qualities, you have truly found a once-in-a-lifetime friend. I have a friend like this; she listens well and gives great advice. She is always ready to help when there is a need. When I am going through hard times, she is there to listen and be supportive. She will gently challenge me, but always with love. When you find a friend like this, you have found a treasure.

God Whispered: I am this type of friend for you. I will never leave you or forsake you. You can always count on me to be there for you, no matter what. You know you can come to me just as you are. I know the desires of your heart. I know you inside and out and I will always be there for you. Keep your heart open to me and you will receive more and more of my love.

"I don't think we realize just how fast we go until you stop for a minute and realize just how loud and how hectic our life is, and how easily distracted you can get."

Meg Ryan

Words to Ponder: I have often been referred to as the "nun on the run." Over the years, I have felt a lot like Martha, busy about many things; but as I grow older, I am becoming more like Mary, spending time sitting at the feet of Jesus, in silence, so I can hear what I may be called to do. Take some quiet time today, for it is only in silence that we can hear the Spirit whisper.

God Whispered: I want you to take time with me. I didn't make you a "human doing" but rather a "human being." I want you to be content with me, without feeling you have to always produce. I love you the way you are. Enjoy your time with me. Continue to rest in my presence.

"I had many teachers who were great, positive role models and taught me to be a good person and stand up and be a good man. A lot of the principles they taught me still affect how I act sometimes, and it is 30 years later."

Kevin James

Words to Ponder: Kevin James stars in the television series "King of Queens." Each episode allows you to laugh at him, and some of the crazy things he has done, but it also helps you to reflect on your own life. He has a great sense of humor and certainly knows how to celebrate life. When we pause for a moment, we remember things our teachers and parents taught us about being a positive role model. Are you a good role model for others?

God Whispered: Each person I send into your life will teach you something about who you are. Listen closely to what they say and watch what they do. I want you to become the best version of yourself. I want you to be happy and proud of what you have accomplished.

"We must make the world a place where: love dominates our hearts, nature sets the standard for beauty, simplicity and honesty are the essence of our relationships, kindness guides our actions, and everyone respects one another."

Susan Polis Schultz

Words to Ponder: Wouldn't it be wonderful if we all lived by this statement! If "love dominates our hearts," then all of these qualities can exist. Can you imagine what a world this would be if: love, beauty, simplicity and honesty, kindness and respect dominated our actions? Certainly the way we treat others is a reflection of the relationship we have with God. God will give us the grace needed to live these qualities.

God Whispered: As you grow in grace you will be transformed into the person I desire you to become. You can possess all these qualities if you are willing to change some of your ways. Change can trigger anxiety and be painful, so cling to me and I will never let go. I love you and want the best for you. If you pay close attention, you will always hear my gentle whispers in your heart.

"To be yourself in a world that is constantly trying to make you something else is the greatest accomplishment."

Ralph Waldo Emerson

Words to Ponder: I remember my dad telling me when I decided to enter the convent: "Don't let them change who you are, they can sand off the rough edges, but if you have to change who you are, that is not a call from God." If someone loves you, they should love you with all your strengths and weaknesses. Sometimes people want to make you into their image and likeness rather than accepting that you were made in God's image and likeness. In today's world, being yourself isn't easy. However, when you are true to the person that God created you to be, you will have peace and fulfillment.

God Whispered: When I created you, I had something special in mind. I want you to become the person I intended you to be. Yes, there are things you may need to change, but I will work with you on these. I am happy that you will do your best to be a reflection of me to the world.

**"Your best friend is the person who brings out
the best that is within you."**

Henry Ford

Words to Ponder: Good friends should help bring out the best in each other. While we accept and love each other as we are, with all our shortcomings and weaknesses, we also encourage each other to become the best we can be. We believe in each other, help each other, and treat each other as we want to be treated – in a respectful, loving way. Having good friends gives us the courage to try new things even though we know we might fail, because we know regardless of the outcome, we still will be loved.

God Whispered: I want you to live life fully. When you love and care for others you make me very happy. I have chosen you to be a reflection of me to those you meet. Consciously rely on me to give you the grace and strength to reach out to others and help them be the best they can be. Trust that I will never leave you.

**"Our greatest happiness does not depend
on the condition of life in which chance has placed us,
but is always the result of a good conscience, good
health, occupation, and freedom in all just pursuits."**

Thomas Jefferson

Words to Ponder: This quote is a great reminder that our greatest happiness does not revolve around our possessions, material things or the circumstances in our life. It reminds us that there are many factors that can help us to truly be happy. By learning how to take better care of ourselves (body, mind, and spirit), we have the energy to pursue a meaningful occupation and follow our dreams.

God Whispered: I want our relationship to be saturated in love and grace. You can accomplish anything as long as you depend on me. Nothing will ever separate you from my love. I love you and will be there for you forever. Continue to live a good life and stay connected to me.

"Study the unusually successful people you know and you will find them imbued with enthusiasm for their work which is contagious. Not only are they themselves excited about what they are doing, but they also get you excited. "

Henry Ford

Words to Ponder: Have you ever had the opportunity to work with someone who really loves what they are doing? Their enthusiasm is contagious, and the creative energy and excitement they express draw others into any project. It is amazing to watch how much gets accomplished when enthusiasm is evident. Enthusiastic people are such a gift for all those working around them.

God Whispered: It gives me so much joy when I see you passionate about what you do. To remain joyful, stay connected to me. I will always be there to encourage you. Just remember to take time to thank me for all the wonderful things that happen in your life. All good things come from me.

"There are two ways to live your life. One is as though nothing is a miracle. The other is as though everything is a miracle."

Albert Einstein

Words to Ponder: I hear about miracles every day. People share their stories with me, and I see how God is working in their lives. One woman told me about her daughter who has Cystic Fibrosis. The doctor told her that her daughter, who was only four months old at the time, would not live past nine months. This mom was a woman of faith, and she refused to give up on her child. She never gave up hope, even though she lost jobs because of the number of times she had to take her daughter to see a specialist. Her daughter is now 34 years old, married and has two daughters of her own. Now that's what I call a miracle; especially when you know the life expectancy for a child born with this dreadful disease! I choose to live my life believing in miracles. How about you?

God Whispered: It is your faith and hope in me that I love. I will never abandon you. I am here to help you. Just turn to me and ask. I will be there for you at all times.

"As we express our gratitude, we must never forget that the highest appreciation is not to utter words, but to live by them."

John F. Kennedy

Words to Ponder: When we say kind things to another, it doesn't cost us a thing, but what it does to the other person can be life changing. Some people watch how we live our lives to see if we are genuine, and really live what we say we believe. When we believe something in our heart and live it, people not only notice but they never forget. Every day is a gift when gratitude is a part of it. Let's remember to be thankful for all that we have been given.

God Whispered: Your words must reflect what is in your heart. It will be evident by how you treat others, and how you want others to treat you. I am always here to guide you, and I am delighted to see what you do for others. I am proud of the work you do, and I will bless others by using you as my disciple.

**"From what we get, we can make a living.
What we give, however, makes a life."**

Arthur Ashe

Words to Ponder: There is a woman in our parish who gives generously to everyone. If she hears there is a need for anything, and I mean anything, she will immediately stop and write a check to cover the cost of whatever the need is at the time. She is greatly respected by our faith community and the entire city. I have never heard of her saying no to anyone who has asked for help. Her giving is what makes her life so fulfilling. Yes, she has been blessed with abundance, but not everyone who is blessed with plenty is generous. Giving for her is living life to the fullest.

God Whispered: I have blessed others with plenty of money and not everyone is generous or willing to share. I want you to share what you have with those in need.

"Don't you quit. You keep walking, you keep trying, and there is help and happiness ahead. Some blessings come soon. Some come late. Some don't come until heaven. Trust God and believe in good things to come."

Jeffrey R. Holland

Words to Ponder: I am not a person who gives up easily. When someone tells me it can't be done, for some odd reason, it gives me even more energy to prove to them that it can. Have you heard the saying: "Where there's a will, there's a way"? Don't give up, you can find a way to make it work. If you believe in what you are doing, and it is meant to be, then you will make it happen. Turn to God; God will always guide you.

God Whispered: The only way to get through tough days is to turn to me, reach out for my hand and I will lead you to the place that will bring you happiness. You will experience many challenges, but it is how you deal with them that will make you the strong person you desire to be. You can accomplish anything if you ask for my assistance.

"When the power of love overcomes the love of power the world will know peace."

Jimi Hendrix

Words to Ponder: Have you ever noticed how many stories on the evening news or in the newspaper are about the love of power? Or have you ever worked with someone whose desire is more about power and control than about doing a good job and giving back/serving? In each of these examples, the person has a need to feel important, take over and even seeks notoriety. The person who has the power of love leads differently: they promote peace not division, and they seek answers that can do the most good rather than what is expedient. In all you do, turn to God and you will learn to love the way God intended you to love. It is the only way you will experience peace of mind and heart.

God Whispered: When you truly walk in my presence, I will displace all the worries, insecurities, and fears you struggle with daily. I created you out of love and want you to care about others. Remember, regardless of what happens to you throughout your day, I will stay close to you. I am just a heartbeat away.

**"Love's greatest gift is its ability to make
everything it touches sacred."**

Barbara de Angelis

Words to Ponder: Those who ever came in contact with Jesus always came away feeling better about themselves. We all are called, as Christians, to share the love that we have received. At the end of the day we need to ask: "Does the way we live our life and treat others reflect the goodness and love of God? "

God Whispered: Whenever you show love and kindness to others, you are creating something beautiful and sacred. I want you to turn to me whenever you need strength and help. Walk with me throughout the day trusting that I will respond to your needs. When you open your heart and listen to me, you will live a life full of surprises!

"The most invisible creators I know of are those artists whose medium is LIFE ITSELF: the ones who express the inexpressible— without brush, hammer, clay, or guitar. They neither paint nor sculpt, their medium is their BEING. Whatever their presence touches has increased life. They see and don't have to draw. They are the artist of BEING ALIVE."

J. Stone

Words to Ponder: People who are truly **alive** are people who have a heart of gratitude. One way they express their love is by thanking people for the things they have done. Eventually, both hearts become open to a beautiful relationship. This type of relationship takes courage and requires trust, which is never easy. It always is a risk when we open our heart to another, but love is worth the risk. Continue living every day to the fullest and see life as an adventure, full of meaning. Be true to the person you know you are deep in your heart and your presence will radiate peace.

God Whispered: I created you simply to enjoy life and live it to the fullest. When you have a grateful heart, and express it, you make me happy. I want you to experience all that life has to offer. Keep your heart open and you will be a great artist, one that brings out the best in others.

"Never forget the three powerful resources you always have available to you: love, prayer, and forgiveness."

H. Jackson Brown, Jr.

Words to Ponder: So much of the time we are not aware of what lies within us. We have the power to bring life to others through our love and prayers. When I love you and not resent you or judge you, it can be healing and life-giving. When I pray for you out of love and concern, you may want to change to be the best version of yourself. When we offer forgiveness, healing can take place. When we can forgive others, we are peaceful, and our very presence can bring forth gifts in others.

God Whispered: I have given you a selfless heart. Use it to its full potential. A heart that can forgive and move on, without resentment, is a heart that wants to love like I do. Continue to share with me all the desires of your heart, know what you need, and I will help you are become who I created you to be.

"If a person loves you but doesn't respect you then it cannot be a real love. It is not possible to love them without respecting them."

Amit Kalantri

Words to Ponder: As we grew up, we were taught to believe that, "All people were worthy of respect," and that respect meant: *"to admire, revere, and be considerate of other people's wishes, feelings, rights, and traditions."*

When I look back at my childhood, I realize how much simpler life was then. While I know I would miss some of the technological advances we have today, it often feels like our lives are lived at such a fast pace. We can use our smartphones to get the latest news, Google directions, make a deposit to our bank account, email, text, keep up with our friends on Facebook and Twitter and destroy a reputation by hitting *"Send."*

How can we protect our young people from this kind of hurt? Part of growing up is making mistakes, but in today's world the consequences of a mistake are magnified as it can be made public, going viral in a manner of seconds. So often we don't think before we say or do something. A petty argument can become blown out of proportion by disrespectful comments or unkind posts made on social network sites. Look at our movies and the television programs today and you will see there is a lack of respect for others. Our churches and schools have begun to address these issues of respect, but we all know that these values must be reinforced in our homes.

God Whispered: My son, Jesus, came to love and never condemned anyone because he or she made a mistake. You see, in the scriptures, how concerned Jesus was with those whom society had ostracized and those who were hurting. Don't you think this should be your mission as well, to be compassionate towards those who fail to meet the mark, and to always be ready to lift up people who are hurting? We must always remember that respect involves all people!

I have taught you to respect everyone no matter what age, race, religion, or life choices. May these five words, "I will never leave you," be a constant reminder that I will be with you no matter what happens to you. I will watch over you, guide you, and love you forever.

"I have not the courage to search through books for beautiful prayers... Unable to say them all or choose between them, I do as a child would do who cannot read – I say just what I want to say to God, quite simply and he never fails to understand."

St. Therese of Lisieux

Words to Ponder: When I wake up in the morning I talk to God without a book in my hand. I start by thanking God for my health, my family, my friends, and my vocation as a religious sister, and the opportunity to serve God's people as a campus minister. Then I ask God to help me to be the person he has called me to be. *"Use me, God; I am yours!"* I share with God my cares and concerns. I ask to have an open heart and trust that he not only knows the desires of my heart but he knows me better than I know myself. He answers my prayers in ways that give me hope and bless me with the courage to take on any task with confidence and love.

God Whispered: I love it when you trust me and are thankful for all the blessings I send your way. When you trust in me, you don't worry. When you concentrate on all your blessings, it keeps you from finding fault with yourself and others. The more you trust in me and the more you turn your life over to me the easier life will be.

"I pray that you all put your shoes under the bed at night so that you gotta get on your knees in the morning to find them. And while you're down there thank God for grace and mercy and understanding."

Denzel Washington

Words to Ponder: Every day that starts with a prayer seems to go better. Our faith is deepened each day as we surrender what we do all day for God. We all have so much to be grateful for. Beginning each day thanking God for our many blessings is an ideal way to start the day. No prayer goes unanswered. The answers may not be what we expect or what we hope, but God continues to speak to us throughout the day. We can't be preoccupied with so many things that we miss the answers. We also need to be free of our preconceptions so we can accept whatever message God gives us.

God Whispered: Come to me with your needs. I want to stay in constant communication with you. I love it when you bring all your concerns to me. The more you trust me, the more abundantly I will bless you and fill your life with a peace you have been wanting. No request is too big.

For me, prayer is a surge
of the heart; it is a simple
look toward heaven, it is
a cry of recognition and
of love, embracing both
trial and joy.

St. Therese of Lisieux

Made in the USA
Charleston, SC
29 September 2015